WHAT EVERY STUDENT SHOULD KNOW ABOUT PROCRASTINATION

August John Hoffman
Compton College and
California State University, Northridge

Boston   New York   San Francisco
Mexico City   Montreal   Toronto   London   Madrid   Munich   Paris
Hong Kong   Singapore   Tokyo   Cape Town   Sydney

Senior Series Editor: Stephen Frail
Series Editorial Assitant: Mary K. Tucker
Executive Marketing Manager: Karen Natale
Production Editor: Claudine Bellanton
Editorial Production Serivce: WestWords, Inc.
Composition Buyer: Linda Cox
Manufacturing Buyer: JoAnne Sweeney
Electronic Composition: WestWords, Inc.
Cover Administrator: Elena Sidorova

For related titles and support materials, visit our online catalog at www.ablongman.com.

To obtain permission(s) to use material from this work, please submit a written request to Allyn and Bacon, Permissions Department, 75 Arlington Street, Boston, MA 02116 or fax your request to 617-848-7320

Between the time website information is gathered and then published, it is not unusual for some sites to have closed. Also, the transcription of URLs can result in typographical errors. The publisher would appreciate notification where these errors occur so that they may be corrected in subsequent editions.

ISBN-10: 0-205-58211-7

Library of Congress Cataloging-in-Publication Data
Hoffman, August John.
  What every student should know about procrastination / August John Hoffman
    p. cm.
  ISBN-13: 978-0-20558211-2
    1. procrastination. 2. Students—Time management. I. Title
BF637.P76H64 2008
155.2'32—dc22

                                             2007026234

Printed in the United States of America

13 14 15 16 17 18 19 20 V036   16 15

Writing this book would have been impossible without the support from my students at Compton College and California State University Northridge. I would also like to thank Stephen Frail and Claudine Bellanton from Allyn & Bacon and Matt Logan of WestWords, Inc. for their help and patience. Finally, I would like to thank my family for providing me with the support and encouragement to continue working when I felt like quitting. I would like to thank my wife Nancy for not allowing me to procrastinate and finish this book, and my children AJ and Sara for waiting "just a few more minutes" after completing each chapter.

CONTENTS

INTRODUCTION

The alarm goes off in your room and you are still exhausted from cramming the night before for an examination. You roll over and press the snooze button for "just 10 more minutes" of sleep. Suddenly you wake up and realize that you are an hour late for class. Now it seems like for the rest of day you simply cannot make any of your appointments on time. Because of your lost time in the morning, you are not able to begin your research project, which is now due in only one week. Suddenly other projects that you had planned on completing later in the day (and later in the week) also don't get accomplished because you can never seem to find the time. A trap develops: the harder you try to get things done, the more you fall behind. You keep putting some things off to try to catch up on the others, but find that you only fall further and further behind. You have lost another day due to poor time management and procrastination. Does this sound familiar to you?

We define procrastination as any negative consequence of delaying, postponing, or simply putting off important projects due to poor time management. We also add a second component to this definition, where the practice of procrastination prevents individuals from becoming *successful* in any endeavor that they pursue. Procrastination is certainly not unique. Almost everyone periodically engages in procrastination, and approximately 20% of individuals may even be classified as chronic procrastinators (*Los Angeles Times* Health Section, January 22, 2007). What makes procrastination most distressing is that in many cases, individuals do have the capacity and skill to complete a particular task but can't, simply because of poor time management skills. Procrastination is less about inherent skill or ability and more about organization, time management and helping you to achieve your goals.

Not finishing something that is irrelevant or unimportant to you (or others) has no real negative consequence. However, when we continuously engage in procrastination involving important projects that may be critical to job performance, your physical health, or academic standing, then the consequences are certainly more relevant. If your doctor tells you to start exercising to avoid a serious health problem, then you would begin exercise right away. A student who has been told by a professor that he or she is in danger of failing the course simply because he or she is not completing assignments on time needs to address and correct the problem of procrastination.

Procrastination is rapidly becoming one of the most significant problems among students relative to their academic performance, as well as employees and workers in private industry. There are several reasons why more and more people are engaging in procrastination. Some people procrastinate due to poor management and organizational skills. Other people procrastinate because of increasing improvements in technology today—computers, the Internet, and text messaging are gobbling up more time now and leaving less time for structured work activities and assignments. Still other people procrastinate because they feel as though they need the "challenge" of working under pressure (usually these people are the ones that turn in incomplete assignments). Whatever the reasons for engaging in procrastination, it is a phenomenon that is rapidly becoming one of the most significant issues in preventing individuals from achieving their goals.

Procrastination and the "Planning Fallacy"

Social psychologists have identified an interesting and very common phenomenon known as the "planning fallacy." The planning fallacy describes some of the reasons why individuals plan so many projects yet fail to complete them in a timely manner (Buehler, Griffin, & Ross, 1994; "Exploring the planning fallacy: Why people underestimate their task completion times," *Journal of Personality and Social Psychology*, 67, 366–381). Researchers explain that the planning fallacy comes from two important suppositions: a) *Planning mode* (an inaccurate assumption of how long a project will take to complete) and b) *Motivation* to complete the project. The concept of the planning fallacy is quite relevant to procrastination. People who engage in procrastination often simply underestimate the magnitude and the complexity of the problem, despite completing similar projects in the past. How often have you known that a project was due and kept putting it off until the last moment because you thought you could do it in a very short time, only to discover that you are out of time? Buehler and his colleagues discovered that a correlation exists between the degree that we *want* to complete a project and the likelihood of our making inaccurate predictions about how long the project will actually take to complete (i.e., "This 10-page term paper should only take me a couple of hours to complete.").

Just *wanting* to complete a project isn't enough to do a good job—individuals must plan ahead and organize their time effectively to give them ample opportunity to complete the best work possible, so that they may begin work with an accurate estimate of how long the project will take to complete. Only when individuals organize and plan properly can they avoid unnecessarily delaying their project or engage in procrastination. Often the primary reason people engage in procrastination is an inaccurate perception of the amount of time required to complete an important project. Think, for example, of an important report that was due. Because you originally thought you could complete it in only one or two days you realized too late that that you grossly underestimated the amount of time necessary to submit a properly completed paper. The end result is that you either turn nothing in on time, or you turn in work that is not at all representative of your true potential and skill.

The "Three S's" of Procrastination: Styles, Situations and Solutions

The purpose of this book is first, to help you identify if you are, in fact, a procrastinator (surprisingly, many people are not even aware that they procrastinate!) and second, to organize and manage your time more effectively to prevent future cases of procrastination. Perhaps the more accurate question is not "Do I procrastinate?" but rather "*How much* do I procrastinate?" To some degree, we all procrastinate on a daily basis. You may delay brushing your teeth until a television program is over, or you may decide to postpone gardening work until after breakfast. While these minor behaviors technically amount to some degree of procrastination, there are no real negative consequences to maintaining a healthy lifestyle or letting your teeth wait a half hour. However, procrastination becomes more serious when the habit of putting things off becomes chronic, and they never get around to doing those important things in their lives.

This book will help you address the problem of procrastination by identifying what type of a procrastinator you are and exploring a number of effective solutions to help you stop.

This book is divided into three simple and easy-to-review sections based on the "Three S's" of procrastination:

- **Styles** of Procrastination. What are the different types of procrastination that people typically engage in?
- **Situations** Involving Procrastination. What are the environments or situations where procrastination seems to develop most readily?
- **Solutions** to Procrastination. What are the methods that are most successful in stopping procrastination?

Styles of Procrastination. Procrastination may take on different forms or styles and people engage in procrastination for different reasons. Some people are highly motivated (a good thing) and take on too many

Figure 1a: The "Three S's" of Procrastination

challenges at once (a bad thing). Some individuals try to cram combine too much work into too little time. They then have to delay completing each project that they have committed to because they simply have over-extended themselves. Others may engage in procrastination due to anxiety or fear of failure in completing the project. Procrastination refers to the inability to complete projects on time due to habitual delaying, but the reasons underlying procrastination are significantly more complex. Often procrastination may result from something as simple as an inaccurate perception of what one actually has control over.

Situations Involving Procrastination. Our second chapter explores the many different types of situations or environments where procrastination is most likely to develop. For example, academic assignments and homework may be delayed due to procrastination, and the likelihood of putting things off keeps growing as more assignments become due. Academics, however, are not the only environment that becomes impacted by procrastination. Other areas include physical health, diet, exercise, and personal relationships.

Solutions to Procrastination. Our third and final chapter explores perhaps the most important segment of our text: the solutions to procrastination. Just as there are several different ways in which procrastination may manifest itself, there are several different solutions to it.

Why Should I Be Concerned about Procrastination?

Everyone should be concerned about procrastination because it negatively influences everyone's lives in some way. In some cases our poorly planned choices (or simply the *lack* of making a choice) may be a causal factor in the development of procrastination (a "procrastination perpetrator"), or a bad decision might be the effect of prior procrastination. In other cases individuals may fail to see other methods that are available in completing projects in a timely manner. In any case, procrastination costs us time, money and personal happiness. The consequences may range from poor performance on an academic project, to an unhealthy lifestyle, or cost us money in the business sector (i.e., delayed contracts or projects not being completed on time).

The relationship between procrastination and how we feel about ourselves is reciprocal. In some situations, we may delay or postpone behaviors simply because we may lack the self-confidence that we think we need, whereas in other situations the delaying (and ultimate failure) of our projects may cause the drop in self-esteem and self-confidence. Procrastination, therefore, has a profound influence not only in how we feel about ourselves but also in how we carry out and execute important responsibilities in our lives. For example, people may delay completing a difficult assignment because they have convinced themselves that they do not have the capacity or aptitude to accomplish their goal. Someone who has experienced difficulty in math may tell themselves: "I just am not any good at math" and prevent themselves from achieving success because they now believe that they lack the capacity to be successful in math. Thus, procrastination may be linked to faulty or inaccurate belief systems of what one has control over (what some psychologists call *attribution theory*—something we will discuss later in this book). We will review several common problems involving procrastination and we will also review proven methods to overcome procrastination. We will begin by summarizing the three basic areas covered by this text:

Different Types of Procrastination

I *Styles* of Procrastination

- Over-ambition (the Overachiever);
- The "Compulsive" Procrastinator;
- The Fantasizer;
- The Underachiever;
- "It's Not My Fault"–External Attribution ;
- "I Just Can't Do It"–Negative Belief Systems

Continued

Where Does Procrastination Typically Occur?

II *Situations* Involving Procrastination
- Academic;
- Professional;
- Health and Physical Issues;
- Personal–Emotional States of Well-Being;

Resolving Procrastination: How to Finish It!

III *Solutions* to Procrastination
- Planning;
- Prioritizing;
- Performing

1

STYLES OF PROCRASTINATION

We have described procrastination as the tendency to delay or postpone projects to the point where our performance at work, school or even our health may become jeopardized. Before we can address the problem, we must first identify the different styles of procrastination. Perhaps one of the most common forms of procrastination is that of the "perfectionist": unrealistically high standards of behavior that prevent you from completing your work, because you fear that it is never good enough. There is a second element here that is also important. To say that you did not finish your project on time because it "wasn't good enough" or "up to my standards" is similar to the fisherman who does not catch a fish all day, and then explains that he or she "ran out of time." The point is that we all have time lines to work under, and the end result of procrastination is the same—incomplete work.

The Perfectionist Procrastinator: Work can never be finished because it can always be improved.

What is a perfectionist? A perfectionist refers to someone who has (unrealistically) high levels or standards of performance and makes excessive demands upon him- or herself regarding the quality of work that they produce. Work must always be "just right" or it isn't good enough. A perfectionist may or may not complete his assignments on time; however, the perfectionist procrastinator is the individual who delays completing his or her project due to constant revisions and changes made to the project that prevent the project itself from being completed. The perfectionist procrastinator typically does not turn in projects on time not because of a lack of skill or competency (quite the contrary, as they are typically more than skilled and competent), but rather due to an inability to accept work done in a satisfactory manner.

Perfectionist procrastinators always start with the best of intentions—they continually refine and revise projects thinking that the more they revise, the better the project. Similar to the alcoholic that promises "just one more drink" the perfectionist procrastinator promises "just one more revision or change and then it will be perfect!" Unfortunately, that final, last time never arrives because the changes are nonstop.

The problem with perfectionist procrastination is that the goal is never achieved because the work itself can always be improved. Typically, perfectionists become frustrated with the quality of their work and continually change their work in an effort to improve their projects. It is important to understand that the perfectionist delays his or her work as a means of avoiding failure. It is much easier to accept a failure by saying that your work was incomplete than to say you tried your best and still failed.

Simply wanting to do the best job that you can do, regardless of the type of work is fine in itself—this is not considered to be perfectionism. Healthy striving and diligence becomes counterproductive and borders on perfectionism when individuals compromise the quality of their work with unrealistic expectations that ultimately result in the work remaining incomplete.

How can you identify the differences between healthy goal setting and perfectionism? Here are a few things to consider:

Healthy Versus Unhealthy Goal Setting Behaviors
- The competent and task efficient individual realizes his or her goals and identifies healthy standards of achievement—they know when to begin and when to end an important project. The perfectionist procrastinator, on the other hand, creates unrealistic expectations in his or her work and expects others to conform to those unrealistic expectations. What may be a realistic goal for one person may not be realistic for

another—Know your skill, potential and skills before identifying a target date to complete a project;

- Task efficient individuals remain structured—they have key factors that indicate progress and are realistic in their goals as they achieve progress. Perfectionists may get distracted by details and the constant desire to start fresh.
- The task efficient individual views success and failure as an integral part of learning—failure of a task simply represents an opportunity for learning in the future. Failure for this person is not necessarily viewed as a negative factor but one where learning occurs. The perfectionist procrastinator demands perfection and has an unrealistic expectation of the quality of his or her work as well as that of others;

Perfectionist Procrastinator Test

Are you a perfectionist procrastinator? If this style of procrastination sounds familiar, then perhaps you may want to take our Perfectionist Procrastinator Test (the "PPT"):

On a scale from "1" to "5" where a score of:
1 = Absolutely Not True;
2 = Somewhat Not True;
3 = Unsure / Don't Know;
4 = Somewhat True;
5 = Absolutely True

1. It is always wrong not to try my hardest at everything I do. ____

2. I need to be in control of events in my life most of the time. ____

3. If something cannot be done at a near-perfect level, then it simply should not be done at all. ____
4. It is okay to keep delaying a project as long is it keeps getting better. ____
5. I tend to focus more on my mistakes than my accomplishments. ____
6. How other people view me influences how I feel about myself. ____

7. I do not like it when people can see my weak points. ____

Continued

8. If I am not giving my full 100% effort in any type of task, I tend to get frustrated, irritable and upset with myself. _____
9. I firmly believe that most people are capable of accomplishing much more in their lives than what they are currently achieving now. _____
10. People who suffer from various types of problems in life (i.e., depression, obesity, anxiety) have the capacity to change—they just haven't discovered how to do it yet. _____

Now add up all of your scores. If your scores fall in the range of:

40–50 = Extreme Perfectionist Procrastinator;
30–39 = Moderate Perfectionist Procrastinator;
20–29 = Low Perfectionist Procrastinator;
10–19 = Not a Perfectionist Procrastinator.

Resolution of Perfectionist Procrastination: Establish realistic goals and structure your time effectively! Strive for balance!

How can you avoid the trap of perfectionism? Set clear and realistic standards to striving for and then move on to other realistic goals. Before beginning any assignment, the perfectionist procrastinator needs to predetermine a specific block of time to complete the project and then turn in the project—no matter what. Break up your work projects and assignments into simple assignments and learn to stop for a break. Decide ahead of time how many revisions you are allowed to do and then move on to the next assignment. Additionally, the perfectionist procrastinator has difficulty in accepting and appreciating accomplishments because they perceive their work typically as "a work in progress" where the work is never complete nor is it ever done ultimately the way they want it done. The perfectionist procrastinator must learn to structure his or her time wisely and accept healthy criticisms of their work. Striving for balance means learning how to devote time to a variety of important activities in your life that promote happiness and well-being. Other suggestions for learning to cope with perfectionist qualities include:

- *Create Time Limits.* Create a schedule or a block of time where you have specifically allocated time for a variety of daily activities. For example, allow yourself 2 to 3 hours for homework (or any project) and then move on to other important activities;

- *Set Realistic Goals.* Identify the realistic advantages to having high standards of work as compared to unrealistic expectations of work that are typically associated with the perfectionist procrastinator. Next, make a list of the advantages (as well as the disadvantages) of perfectionism. For example, you might say that perfectionism always yields exceptional qualities of work—but the disadvantage may be that the work is always extended and often incomplete;
- *Know When to Say Enough!* Always set time limits on your work—even if you have to finish your work and you think you could have done a better job if you had more time. The point is that you finished something and that you are moving beyond the primary problem of procrastination.

The Compulsive ("Overachiever") Procrastinator

There are many phrases that describe effort as a very positive trait or characteristic, such as "if at first you don't succeed" or "You can achieve anything you want if you only try hard enough." For the person who believes these phrases to be literally true, they may be working excessive hours and trying to take on too many responsibilities that may ultimately impact not only the quality of their work but the likelihood of on-time completion. Often procrastination is simply due to poor planning and organizational skills. Overachievers may easily become procrastinators because of their tendency take on more work than they can achieve in the allotted time. The topic of being an "overachiever" has many similar components to the "perfectionist procrastinator."

For example, an overambitious procrastinator may keep on revising and rewriting a term paper to the point that it becomes overdue, or they may "cram" and study for several hours refusing to take a break The overambitious procrastinator (similar to the perfectionist procrastinator) needs to learn to channel their drive and develop structure in their routines so they may meet deadlines for their projects.

In many situations involving procrastination, individuals want to excel and succeed so much that they try to do too many things at once, and unfortunately are unable to complete any of them at the highest level possible. With the overambitious individual, the problem is that they often (willingly) take on numerous tasks and projects that far exceed their ability to complete them in a satisfactory manner. They typically begin to procrastinate or put off completing projects because they do not know where to start or what is due first.

Resolution of the Overachiever Procrastinator

Identify your limits and be realistic about what types of projects you can complete on time. It is far better to complete one or two assignments on time and do a great job than to try to complete eight or ten jobs in a very unsatisfactory manner.

- Identify your strengths and goals—be clear in terms of knowing how much time you have in order to meet each goal.

The Fantasizer or "Pie in the Sky" Procrastinator

Creativity and the effects produced by an individual's imagination can be wonderful components to an individual's work and can certainly add to the quality of one's career. Some of the most prolific writers have had incredible imaginations where they put their ideas into their works (such as literature) and have utilized their capacity for fantasy in a very productive and resourceful way. Stephen King, Isaac Asimov, and Ernest Hemingway are examples of very famous authors who have had the capacity to capture the rich quality of their imagination and write in a way that the reader may be both entertained and enthralled. However (and here is the link with procrastination) the key point is that these individuals were able to make their fantasies actually *work* for them and put their ideas to constructive use. Unfortunately, many individuals who engage in chronic fantasizing are not that driven or fortunate. When we "fantasize" we dream about how things "could be" in our lives and unfortunately never act on these dreams.

The fantasizer procrastinator shows tremendous creativity, imagination and diversity in his or her behaviors; however, their ability to carry out or execute projects on time is severely limited. Success means more than being gifted in one or several ways—success often means having the ability to meet deadlines and work systematically towards a specific goal. Ask any teacher or professor of higher education and most will agree that persistence and determination are ultimately the key ingredients to success—not simply being an academic prodigy.

The fantasizer has tremendous capacity for dreaming but lacks the ability to think in concrete and realistic concepts that involve time management, deadlines, and meeting goals. The fantasizer requires structure and "reality checks" from time to time to make sure that they are aware when projects are due. Additionally, they appear to become involved in their own world and tend to disregard deadlines imposed by others. Often some of the most successful entrepreneurs are highly creative individuals who tend to "think outside the box." However, the fantasizer procrastinator fails to understand that creative and successful individuals are able to integrate the realities of deadlines with their assignments and produce exceptional work that is also done on time.

The energy and capacity for establishing original concepts among fantasizers is exceptional—often types of employment involving fantasizers includes artists and musicians because they tend to create their own original work without the constraints of "realistic" limitations. However, the most successful artists are those who can manage both their flights of fancy and their deadlines.

Resolution of the Fantasizer Procrastinator

We have described the advantages of a creative mind and how the use of fantasy can actually enhance the quality of an individual's work. However, unless the individual who actually engages in fantasizing is capable of remaining structured and organized, then usually work is delayed and procrastination is the end result. Time management is perhaps the single most important thing that individuals need to consider when trying to eliminate procrastination. The fantasizer procrastinator usually has more than enough time to complete his or her project. The problem with those who tend to fantasize about projects is that they spend so much time thinking, they run out of time to actually apply their ideas to the project.

How can the individual who engages in fantasizing stop his or her procrastination tendencies? Here are a few suggestions:

- *Set Concrete Goals.* Identify clearly what your goals are before beginning your project and then select a finish date. Fantasizing what you would like to develop in your life is fine, but always make sure that your goals are realistic and concrete. Pick a date when your project will be completed and determine a plan to achieve it.

- *Creating Contracts.* A contract is a written statement that clearly delineates your goals and how they will be achieved. Contracts should be written in a very clear and direct manner outlining what will happen when your goals are met on time (i.e., rewards) or consequences for not completing goals on time. (See below for an example of an effective contract with an individual who wishes to improve his or her physical health by using a contract to report to a gym on a regular basis.) Often the fantasizer procrastinator "forgets" about due dates or "loses track of time." The personalized contract will clearly prevent this from happening. Be sure to focus on key elements of your report and the dates when they are due. Finally, be sure to include clear reward systems (i.e., similar to a token economy system) once your goals have been identified:

- *Improving Time Management.* We have stated earlier how important the skills of fantasy and creativity can be and how vital they can be relative to other forms of work. The common problem among those who do engage in fantasy is that they typically need to focus more on applying their ideas to practical problems within a reasonable amount of time. You can have all of the most wonderful ideas in the world, but if you do not apply them within a reasonable period of time, then the ideas become counterproductive.

The Fantasizer Procrastinator Contract

Your contract may look something like this:

I, Mr. / Ms. "Fantasizer Procrastinator," will make a commitment to . . . [List goals here: i.e., report to the gym and work under the supervision of trainer Mary Smith for a period of time of one year; complete report X to supervisor Smith by a specific date]. I will come to the gym at 7:00 am for a minimum of three times a week (Monday, Wednesday, and Friday) and will participate in an aerobic or cardiovascular exercise program for at least 30 minutes, followed by a weight circuit of 20 minutes. Finally, I will complete my exercise program with at least 15 minutes of stretching and "warm down" exercises. Additionally, while participating in this exercise program, I have made a commitment to monitor my caloric intake and have been advised to use a low-carbohydrate diet recommended by my nutritionist. I will treat myself to a (non-food) reward for each week of successful participation— such as going to a movie, visiting my friends, or just making time for myself. I promise to faithfully adhere to these regulations, and if I violate any one of them (i.e., if I decide to "sleep in" one morning or if I eat the wrong foods), I will make a contribution of fifty ($50.00) dollars to any charity that Mary choose each time I violate my contract. I have promised my health trainer Mary, promised to myself, my family and friends to let them know about my decisions to improve my health so they may also offer support to me. This program benefits me and my family. Most importantly, I will make it a point each time I come to the gym to train to have fun, value and use my time wisely.

Signed:	Ted Johnson
Witnessed:	Mary Smith
Date:	February 2007

The "Underachiever" Procrastinator

So far most of our examples involving procrastination have involved individuals who have been overachievers or those who simply try to do too much in too short a time. In some cases, the procrastinator may delay task completion due to excessive day-dreaming (the fantasizer) or experience problems with organization and time management. These problems can typically be addressed by showing these procrastinators how to clearly identify their goals (i.e., through the use of goal setting or contracts) and better manage their time. However, with the classic "underachiever" procrastinator, failure to reach goals may be somewhat more problematic. The underachiever procrastinator fails to complete projects not because of a lack of talent, skill or aptitude, but usually out of pure fear of failure. Unlike the perfectionist, they don't revise or rewrite themselves past their deadlines; unlike the overachiever, they don't take on too much at once; they simply don't try because it is easier to ascribe failure to a lack of concern than it is to admit that they really did want to pass the examination but were unable to do so.

The underachiever protects his or her ego by saying they "could have done it" had they tried or wanted to complete the project. He or she delays and procrastinates in completing the project and as a result fails to complete the assignment. The real challenge here is to try to help the underachiever realize his or her potential and to learn to take risks (i.e., make a commitment where failure is possible) but also to help them to learn from their mistakes so future success is possible. Future success in completing projects in this case means reducing procrastination and taking on new assignments. It is much easier on the ego to simply say "I failed because I didn't really want to pass the exam" or "I failed because I didn't study" rather than saying "I really tried to finish the report (but couldn't)" or worse still: "I really studied hard for that test and still failed." You can see how underachievers really need to work on self-esteem and self-efficacy.

Resolution of the "Underachiever" Procrastinator

The first step in addressing the problems of the underachiever procrastinator would be realizing the underachiever's strengths and weaknesses and making an accurate assessment of his or her potential relative to the task at hand. The fear of failure often stems from the underachiever's uncertainty about his or her potential and skill. Usually when the underachiever procrastinator discovers (or rediscovers) their potential, the tendency to procrastinate is reduced and a willingness to take on new challenges increases.

Start tasks on a small scale.

The underachiever gives up before he or she has even begun. By breaking down projects into smaller tasks and setting easily achievable goals, the underachiever can learn that the steps of the project are not impossible. Completion of smaller tasks also grows the confidence of the underachiever. The underachiever needs to first identify relatively small or short-term goals, work to completion and then be rewarded. Through a gradual process of identifying their strengths underachievers learn to take on greater responsibilities without fear of failure. A key component to this process is the cognitive behavioral approach to shaping. Shaping is described as learning in small steps, where each forward step or progression is acknowledged with some small reward. (See the Step-by-Step Approach below.)

Find areas of strength.

Once underachievers have gained confidence in their ability to successfully complete a task, they can start learning more about their strengths and how to use them. Through time they will be able to take on greater and greater responsibilities to gradually reach their full capabilities.

One of the most effective ways to help the underachiever to realize his or her goals is in creating a short, manageable and realistic program with clear cut rewards after each step has been successfully managed. Similar to the contract used in with the "Fantasizer" procrastinator, the "Step-by-Step" approach is very successful with the underachiever procrastinator, as each goal or step is clearly highlighted and delineated so they know what needs to be done every step of the way. Furthermore, a key component to the Step-by-Step program is that (unlike the contract form used with the fantasizer procrastinator), after each step is successfully mastered, a small reward is offered to maintain focus and the positive momentum needed to complete his or her task. The following sample is a good example of the Step-by-Step Approach:

The Step-by-Step Approach:
Discover Your Potential in Reaching Your Goals!

You have been delaying your psychology report for several weeks now, and you do not want to continue this procrastination. You have decided to begin the project, but it now seems overwhelming, and you only have two weeks left. How can you complete your project and end your procrastination? Creating a classic "Step-by-Step" Approach allows the underachiever to discover his or her strengths in a very methodical, structured and highly effective manner. Used this way, individuals begin tasks (an important first step for underachievers) at their own pace and work to success. With each small step of progress, a small but highly symbolic token of success is given to the individual that will serve to reinforce consistent and continued project until the project is successfully completed.

Below is a sample of a description of an effective "Step-by-Step" Approach with a typical procrastination-related problem with students and completing a research paper:

> **Day 1:** *Identify topic for research paper.* You go to the library and review all topics relative to your chapter addressing human personality. You have decided to select altruism and pro-social behaviors as your topic.
> **Reward:** Going out to dinner with friends;
> **Day 2:** *Conduct literature review for paper.* You select a target number of sample literature reviews for your paper (five to ten different articles related to prosocial behaviors). Contact professor of the course, a tutor or teacher assistant to confirm topic is appropriate and collaborate ideas. This not only assures you that you are on the right track, but it also shows your teacher your levels of motivation and drive in completing your project;
> **Reward:** Going out to movies with friends.
> **Day 3:** *Write rough draft of paper.* Continue working on your paper and revising—give yourself breaks in between;

Reward: Going outdoors for a walk.

Day 4: *Refine your paper.* Review it with your professor for additional information.

Reward: Going out with your friends to dinner.

Day 5: *Final clean draft.* Work submitted on time!

Reward: Have a party! Celebrate your accomplishments.

Step-by-Step Calendar

You can use the blank calendars below for your next projects. Break the tasks into steps that can each be completed in one day. Don't forget your rewards!

"It's Not My Fault!": External vs. Internal Attribution and Procrastination

Perhaps the single most common style of procrastination is the giving up of responsibility for what happens to them or that they feel events occurring within their personal or professional lives are out of their control. These individuals ask the convincing question: "If something is beyond my control, then why bother trying to change it?" Earlier research conducted by Bernie Weiner at UCLA (Weiner, 1993, 1995) addressed three key factors in understanding attribution theory: How stable situational factors are, how controllable or uncontrollable circumstances are, and internal (it's my own fault) versus external attributions ("The dog ate my homework.")?

Here are some very common statements made by individuals who engage in an external attribution relative to problems in their lives:

- "If I am genetically predisposed to be overweight, then why should I bother to start a healthy exercise program?"
- "If I am predisposed to suffer from alcoholism, then it really isn't my fault if I continue to abuse alcohol."
- "If math is just too hard for me or if I have a math phobia (dyscalculia) then it is okay for me to stop trying to improve my math scores."

These arguments are very convincing—they may often make compelling statements and we may empathize with them on a variety of topics. However, ultimately the responsibility of stopping smoking, reducing weight, improving your GPA, finishing a report, or whatever your goal is lands on your shoulders. When people typically find reasons why they cannot meet their expectations and successfully complete their goal, they often create reasons (i.e., "extenuating circumstances") to justify their failure.

What Is "Internal" or "External" Attribution?

The term *internal attribution* (often called "internal locus of control") was originally introduced by Rotter (1965) to describe the perception of what we feel we have control over in our lives. Conversely, the term *external attribution* (or "external locus of control") refers to our perception of what we lack control over. Individuals who maintain higher levels of external attribution often show significantly higher levels of depression, lower self-esteem, and general unhappiness within the context of their relationships with others. Higher levels of internal attribution are positively correlated with success, happiness, and a sense of autonomy. Note that having an internal locus of control does not guarantee success with every task, but individuals typically report feeling more satisfied in knowing that they have the capacity to master and understand most events occurring within their life. How do you know if you have an internal or an external locus of control? Try taking this simple test to see if you believe that you have the power and capacity to control the majority of events in your life:

"My Destiny or My Choice" Questionnaire:
To What Degree Do We Control The Outcomes of Our Lives?

Answer each of the questions below. Score each answer with either:

    1 = Absolutely Not True;
    2 = Somewhat Not True;
    3 = Not Sure / Don't Know
    4 = Somewhat True; and
    5 = Absolutely True

1. Sometimes I feel that no matter how hard I try to do something, it is inevitable that I fail. _____
2. I generally believe that all people are "born a certain way," meaning that things are going to happen to you no matter what and you should bother trying to change your destiny. _____
3. Usually when I fail at something I don't bother trying again because I typically will fail again. _____
4. It is hard for me to change certain things in my life because it is just the way I am. _____
5. I believe that if someone does something good or bad in their life they will usually be rewarded or punished for it later on in their life. _____

6. I think that some people just have better or worse luck than others. _____
7. How well I perform in school (or work) is really a matter of chance or bias on the part of my teacher (or employer). _____
8. Most problems people really cannot plan for or control. _____
9. If someone rejects my ideas or argues with me, I usually give in to him or her. _____
10. I tend to be superstitious—sometimes I have good days an sometimes I have bad days and there is really little that I can do about it. _____

Now add up your scores. If your scores fall in the range of:

40–50: Fatalist/Determinist—Very Strong Perceptions of External Attribution. Those individuals scoring within this range believe that they have very little control over important events within their life. Change is considered to be very difficult for individuals who score within this range.

30–39: Partial Determinist—Moderate Perceptions of External Attribution. There is a belief in *some* minimal control over events occurring within your life. The partial determinist believes that individuals have little (but some) actual control over their lives. Change is possible, but comes at a cost. Partial determinists often cite "genetic tendencies" to engage in a variety of behaviors and argue that behaviors are primarily genetically influenced—indicating a primary lack of control of the events that may happen to us. For example, the partial determinist may not fault the individual who is convicted of drunk driving for the fourth time in five years because of his or her genetic inheritance of the predisposition or the "disease.";

20–29: Limited Free Will—Mixed Perceptions of Internal Attribution. Individuals scoring within this range feel that their behaviors are primarily a "mix" between what they have learned (free will) and genetically inherited predispositions to some behaviors. Individuals here always accept primary responsibility for their behaviors, but also consider extenuating variables, such as inheritance and genetics.

10–19: Primary Free Will—Very Strong Perceptions of Internal Attribution. Individuals scoring at this range believe in absolute and full authority and autonomy of their own behaviors. They tend to view failure as primarily their fault and look for ways to learn from past mistakes. All things are within their control and their belief is that society would be much better if all persons accepted full responsibility for their own behaviors.

"I Just Can't Do It": Negative Belief Systems and Procrastination

Cognitive strategies (or belief systems) often influence our behaviors by affecting what we think we can or cannot do relative to a specific task. Our belief system often controls what we do by suggesting what we think we are capable of achieving. For example, a student with only modest academic skills may not apply to a highly competitive graduate school, or an athlete who can run at a moderate pace may not try to break any records in endurance. An overweight individual may not attempt to change eating habits and diet if they feel that losing weight is impossible for them. Conversely, individuals that feel that weight loss is possible are more likely to lose weight permanently because they feel they are in control of various outcomes in their life.

Procrastinators often have an erroneous belief system about what they actually have control over, as well as their own aptitude and skills. Stated in simpler terms—Negative thoughts tend to elicit negative or destructive behaviors. How many times have you heard someone say that they are "just really bad at doing something"— regardless of what the actual task really is? How many times have you heard other students or friends complain about their perceived failure at a given task and then summarize by saying that they just are inherently bad at performing math skills or physical activities of some sort? When we justify our failures by (inaccurately) concluding that we are naturally inept at a particular behavior we are creating excuses for not persevering to success and thus continue the process of procrastination by not taking proactive measures to eliminate the problem.

Most importantly, procrastinators need to understand that they do have control over external factors, and do have the power to change our skill and aptitude levels. There are actually very few things in our lives where we lack all control in the outcome, including our physical health, our levels of activity, and our levels of communication. Arguably we have some control over our employment (we may choose our own career but may be denied a promotion or raise), being accepted to any variety of schools, or the types of relationships with others we choose to have with others.

By continuously criticizing your own performance you are creating a handicap for yourself in future activities. The cognitive theorists argue that if you want success, then you need to think success in several ways. People who suffer from depression or those who are chronic procrastinators rarely engage in positive thinking and often rationalize or justify their own forms of procrastination by creating negative thought patterns. Common examples include:

- *Your Future and Your Career.* Applying to one or two competitive graduate schools where the applicant is rejected: "I'll never get in to any graduate school—I may as well quit school now" or
- *Your Personal Health.* Trying to diet to lose weight and being unsuccessful the first time: "I tried to lose weight but was unsuccessful—I am destined to be overweight my whole life . . . I tried, it didn't work, so why bother to continue to try?"
- *Unhealthy Habits.* "I smoke cigarettes because I enjoy it, not because I can't quit" or "I am addicted to junk food."
- *Your Personal and Intimate Relationships with Others.* Breaking up in a relationship with a loved one and telling yourself that you are "destined to be alone, miserable and unhappy the rest of your life" because of one failed relationship.
- *Your Academic Performance.* Telling yourself that you are never going to be able to understand a difficult chemistry or math course. You have convinced yourself that "good mathematicians are born . . . not made."

Often when individuals engage in negative thought patterns they also tend to elicit either negative or pessimistic views about themselves and the world around them. They may further engage in procrastination by avoiding their responsibilities caused by the depression. Thus, a vicious cycle develops where individuals become depressed because of their negative thoughts and pessimistic views pertaining to their lives, and because of their depression they continuously procrastinate their responsibilities. The more they procrastinate, the more depressed they become, and because of increased depression, the less likely they are to begin work and stop procrastination. At some point, the individual must simply "Stop!" the pessimism, depression and procrastination.

Resolution of the Maladaptive Cognitive Strategies Procrastinator: Start Thinking Positive Thoughts!

Earlier in this section we described negative thoughts as being related to procrastination, where if you think you cannot complete a specific project or task, then you will not complete that project. Individuals who suffer from a variety compulsive behaviors (i.e., gambling, overeating, or substance abuse) may feel out of control and unable to stop them. They may even believe that they have "genetic predispositions" or internal factors that somehow force them to engage in these counterproductive behaviors. The simplest and easiest way to stop unhealthy behavior and engage in healthy or productive behaviors is to first think positively that you can change the behavior and then make the changes in a structured format. The person who engages in procrastination typically thinks that the project for them to complete is somehow impossible and that they need to delay the project (procrastinate) to give them more time to complete the project. Unfortunately, what will typically happen is continued procrastination and a continued belief in negative thoughts. Change the unhealthy or counterproductive thought into a productive one and the behaviors will change: **No more procrastination.**

2

SITUATIONS INVOLVING PROCRASTINATION

Any environment that regulates work productivity is capable of providing opportunities for procrastination. The four most common areas of procrastination include educational environments (i.e., schools where assignments are due), the employment environment, personal lifestyles, and physical health. We will first begin our discussion addressing the environment where procrastination is most likely to occur—school work.

Academic Procrastination

If you are a student, think for a moment after reading this paragraph how many times has this type of event occurred to you: You know that you have a report that has been due for some time but you have delayed starting it and now it is due in three days. You delay and postpone in completing your project, and finally when you only have two days left you produce a very mediocre or unsatisfactory paper. You complete the project, but you typically tell yourself what a "better job I could have done if I only had more time." You are probably right—you most certainly could do a much better job if you had more time. *What you need to realize is that you did have enough time—you just chose not to use it wisely!* Why do you (and so many others) do this to yourselves? A significant aspect of success in academics is in planning, structure, and the organization of work. Procrastination can occur just about anyplace that you can imagine, such as in school where you have frequently been avoiding an important project or assignment.

Procrastination in the Workplace

If you are employed and working at any type of job that involves deadlines, then you know how important it is to keep them. Individuals who procrastinate often limit themselves from professional development and learning skills by delaying important projects. In the professional world the ramifications and negative consequences of procrastination can be even more detrimental than they are for students. Not turning in work such as accounts or important reports on time can result in negative reviews, demotions or even dismissal from your place of employment. Given the fact that most people actually spend more time at work than they spend with the own families, it is imperative that individuals in the professional world learn how not to procrastinate and how to improve their job performance.

Health and Physical Issues

The area in our lives that is perhaps most susceptible to the problem of procrastination is that of our physical health, wellness, and exercise. For whatever reason, exercise has unfortunately taken on a very negative image (especially among adolescents and children) that involves excruciating work, sweat and pulled muscles. These common (albeit incorrect) images of exercise have perhaps contributed to the inherent problem of procrastination and maintaining a health or exercise program.

Many individuals begin a new year, a new job or go back to school after several years with very ambitious goals in mind. Unfortunately, if we are not structured in our time and set specific and realistic goals, we either fail to achieve those goals or never begin them in the first place. Most individuals who make a New Year's resolution give up in February. Why are personal health commitments and contracts so frequently abandoned? The reason is that most people delay beginning their program and by the time they start they are unsure how to continue. A personal health program may begin with a contract or a commitment to a friend or family member who will provide you the support you need to be successful in your efforts.

How does procrastination influence levels of our physical health? Imagine that you have made a contract with yourself to improve your health by exercising three times a week. You know you need to exercise, and you even want to exercise, but each time that you are about to begin, something else always happens to be in the way—you delay and delay your program until now you are not just 10 lbs. overweight, but 20 lbs. overweight. Where does it all stop? How can you regain control in your life and stop procrastinating?

Personal—Emotional States of Well-Being

Are you the kind of person who is always doing things for others but often neglect the things that you need to do in your own life? Do you delay and postpone important things for yourself because of a commitment to help your family or friends? How often have you decided to do something positive just for yourself—perhaps going on a vacation, or just taking time off to relax from work, but always other things keep getting in the way? Your "dream time" and personal time for yourself keeps escaping you, and you find yourself procrastinating about taking time off for yourself. A final important area of procrastination involves individuals who delay in making time for themselves to relax and unwind. Personal and emotional wellness is critical to healthy and productive living. Many people today are living very hectic and busy lifestyles where attention to their personal health (i.e., relaxation) and physical health becomes neglected. It is very easy to put off, delay and procrastinate for ourselves because we think we can do without a break or vacation. An important component of healthy and effective living is structuring time and responsibilities evenly where our emotional needs are taken care of.

3

SOLUTIONS TO PROCRASTINATION: PLANNING, PRIORITIZING & PERFORMING

Our final chapter addresses perhaps the most important issue relative to procrastination—and that is how to stop procrastination so you may successfully complete outstanding projects and move on in your life. Up to this point in our discussion we have addressed what procrastination is (and is not) and we have explored under what different types of circumstances it is most likely to develop. We have also reviewed the different types of procrastinators, everything from the "perfectionist" procrastinator to the "fantasizer" procrastinator. We will now address the problem of procrastination and describe three of the most effective solutions to procrastination:

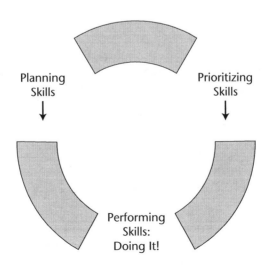

Planning
Skills

Prioritizing
Skills

Performing
Skills:
Doing It!

How Planning Prevents Procrastination

Perhaps the single most frustrating experience for people who frequently engage in procrastination is that they often feel *capable* of completing projects and *competent* in doing their work assignments, but somehow lack the drive and the organizational skills that will facilitate their ability to complete their projects. In other words, task completion is more about organization, structure and perseverance than it is about natural or inherent ability. The ability in completing tasks correctly comes with a very sound and structured approach where you not only know *what* to do, but more importantly *when to do it*. While there are several different types of procrastinators, there is one common denominator: lack of organizational skills. Our chapter on the solutions to—and preventions of—procrastination will address the "Three P's of Procrastination": Planning, Prioritizing and Performing. Planning out your projects means that you have identified exactly what needs to be done, prioritizing your projects means that you have identified when each project is going to be done, and finally performing each project means actually engaging in the task itself and accomplishing your goals.

Planning Skills: *Achieving Structure: Stay Focused & Stay Organized*

Procrastinators usually have problems in planning ahead and completing assignments and responsibilities because they lack the ability to identify when certain projects need to be completed by a specific date. Procrastinators also tend to live in the "here and now" and often neglect or ignore their future or the ramifications of their behaviors on the future. Without organization and structure, you have no way of identifying "low-priority" projects from "high-priority" projects.

For example, a common problem that occurs with those who engage in chronic procrastination is in allowing all (or most) of their assignments and projects to "pile up" at once so that they face several deadlines simultaneously. For students, this is especially true during their final exams, or with employees who work in any kind of reporting cycle. A good plan identifies the overall goal of a project and breaks it down into individual steps, with realistic timeframes for the completion of each step. Identifying which step should come first is part of prioritizing, the next step in avoiding procrastination.

Prioritizing: *What Needs to be Done First?*

It is very easy to see how the individual who frequently engages in procrastination postpones important projects. Many different types of projects begin to develop and deadlines seem to appear all at once. Things soon begin to become overwhelming and many people simply do not have any idea where to begin first, and then they feel helpless and out of control. Prioritizing your schedule can prevent this state of thing from ever occurring in the first place. What is most important to you? What needs doing right now and what is the best manner to go about doing it? Here is a sample of a schedule that needs organizing and prioritizing and see if you can identify what things should be done first:

> Tim is a 20 year old psychology major who lives in an apartment off campus. He lives by himself and his apartment has not been cleaned in over a month. He works part-time at the school library and his supervisor has requested that he sort the 800 books that are sitting in the library basement in the next week. Tim is currently carrying a full load of units this semester. He has gotten somewhat behind in his school work and has an examination in biology next week (Monday, February 15), a research paper in psychology due in one month (March 15), and his employer at the school library has requested a work schedule for the next three months. In addition to these projects, Tim has been putting off taking his car in for some minor repairs and has promised his friends that he would begin going to the gym with them on a regular basis. Tim is now overwhelmed with his school work and his responsibilities at the library.

In order to stop procrastinating, Tim first needs to prioritize—what is most important and needs to be done first? In the space below, identify all of the listed items that need to be addressed by Tim, and then prioritize or arrange in order what needs to be done first:

Project #1: _____

Project #2: _____

Project #3: _____

Project #5: _____

Project #6: _____

How to Prioritize Your Goals: Defeating Procrastination

When we prioritize our goals we are arranging different types of events in order—how can you determine what needs to be done first? In some situations the answer is obvious. Doing a required term paper that constitutes 25% of your course grade should clearly take precedence over doing your laundry. Unfortunately, prioritizing goals with clearly defined deadlines is usually not so easy. In the above exercise about Tim, what do you think should be done first?

There are six clearly defined activities that Tim needs to complete. Some of these activities can wait, whereas others are urgent. Some students place a score indicating the rank of priority for each task. For example, a score of "1" may indicate urgent attention; a score of "2" may indicate important; a score of "3" may indicate moderate importance, and so on. If we can summarize all of Tim's tasks, we see the following:

- Tim needs to study for a Biology examination in one week—because of the deadline rapidly approaching, this should take priority #1;
- Tim's supervisor at the library indicated that he needs to get busy and sort over 800 books in about two weeks. Because this job is Tim's only source of income, his employment takes priority #2;
- Tim needs reliable transportation, and his car has been making some funny noises lately. Tim is certain that the car needs a simple tune up, and thus car maintenance takes priority #3

(note: If the car problem had been serious, such as braking problems, this would take first priority for safety reasons);

• Tim has another academic assignment due, however, this assignment isn't due until one month. For this reason, the research paper has been given Priority #4. Tim should select a date next week to begin work on the report with some of his fellow classmates;

• With all of his attention to school work and completing his responsibilities at the library, Tim has neglected his own personal health. He has gained 15 pounds in the last 6 months, and feels flabby and out of shape. For this reason, exercise and health has been identified as priority #5;

• Finally, Tim's apartment looks very sloppy and neglected. He feels better when his room and apartment is organized, so he has picked a convenient time and date (Sunday at 2:30 pm) to rearrange his apartment and do some major cleaning. Because the apartment cleaning can be done just about anytime with no negative consequences, this has been awarded the lowest priority (#6).

Procrastination and "Chipping": How to Simplify Your Life by Taking Small Steps First

Procrastination begins with people simply putting off assignments to a later and more convenient time. The problem is, however, that there really is no more convenient time for many projects that need to be done in the here and now. In other situations individuals may develop the habit of postponing work assignments simply because they don't know how or where to begin. If you have ever felt overwhelmed with many important projects all due simultaneously, you know how difficult it can be to get a handle on what needs to be done first. In the above example with Tim, we described a method known to reduce procrastination by prioritizing your goals. This method is very advantageous for two reasons: The first is that when you write down everything that needs to be done you have a very clear idea of what each project entails; and the second advantage is that you are able to identify what needs to be done first.

What Is "Chipping"?

A second example of reducing procrastination is through a technique that we refer to as "chipping." Chipping is similar to a strategy called *successive approximation* used in behavioral therapy to help clients who have particular fears (even phobias) of certain places or things. The feared object or place is often first just discussed, then imagined by the client on a gradual basis until he or she can manage to come progressively closer to the thing they fear. Ultimately, the client realizes that the fear is irrational and they can resume their lives in a healthy manner.

In much the same way, "chipping" can work for individuals who often engage in procrastination. People who engage in procrastination are often avoiding their project out of poor time management skills, or else they feel overwhelmed by their project and simply do not know how to begin. Their frustration increases as they delay and continue with their procrastination because their work projects continue to pile up. Does this sound familiar to you? One highly effective method in preventing work assignments from "piling up" is not to try to do everything at once, but rather to slowly (and methodically) begin your work one step at a time—or "chipping away" at what appears to be an insurmountable task.

In chipping we instruct students to simply begin working— starting anywhere so they can at least have a starting point. Once individuals have actually begun their assignment or project, they realize that they can continue and gradually complete their project. Sometimes just knowing that you have finally begun the project that you have been avoiding is very rewarding. Chipping is thus defined as an effective approach to help people reach their goals by breaking down and simplifying complex projects into simpler and more manageable "baby steps." No matter how small the steps are, the individual is gradually achieving his or her goal of task completion. Furthermore, as time progresses people typically feel more confident in their ability to ultimately complete their project in a successful manner.

Often the single most important factor in achieving our goals is in how we pursue them. Let us again resume the example of Tim and his assignments that are due. Tim has to complete a report, prepare for an exam, clean his apartment, and get his car repaired.

If anyone (regardless of their skills) put all of these assignments together at once, they would become overwhelmed and simply throw up their hands in exasperation. They typically would feel unable to meet all the demands at once. But herein lies the key to the chipping method—think of only one project (the most important project) to be completed at once—and only think of that. Once your first project has been completed, then move on to the second, then the third, and so on. Before you realize it, your work will be completed because with each individual assignment being completed you are gaining more self confidence in yourself and you are beginning to feel more empowered to be successful.

Performing: *Just Get It Done!*

The final component to defeating procrastination is perhaps (conceptually) the most simple—*doing* what needs to be done. However, before you perform the tasks that will complete the project you must first identify them (Planning) and then recognize their relative importance (Prioritizing). In the planning section we discussed the importance of structure and organizational skills—knowing not only what to do but how to do it. In the Prioritizing section we learned to recognize how to arrange our tasks in order of importance based on deadlines, other commitments, and even health and safety issues. Prioritizing was the second critical feature of the solutions section. Often people begin to procrastinate simply because everything appears to be important and everything seems to require our attention immediately. Once we have identified a plan of what needs to be done and we have prioritized what should be done first, we are ready for the final portion of the solutions chapter—performing the task. Prioritizing allows individuals to do the most important tasks first and then progress in a hierarchy by completing all other important tasks. Actually performing the task eliminates any possibility of engaging in procrastination. There are four key factors that are associated with performing the task at hand:

- Record your goals: What needs to be done?
- Realistic goals: Assign realistic, attainable goals to boost a sense of accomplishment

---

- ## Record Your Goals
- ## Realistic Goals—Start Small & Work Up to Your own Potential;
- ## Relax—Work at Your Own Pace;
- ## Reward Yourself—Find an Incentive to Complete Your Project

---

- Relax—Find your optimal style or zone of performance and enjoy what you are actually doing.
- Reward yourself—After your goals have been identified and achieved—reward yourself with a predetermined goal (see page 9 on contracts).

By actually performing the task, you are take responsibility for completing that ever important first step. Before actually doing the thing that you have been avoiding, you must first know what should be done. For many people this may be as simple as keeping a list handy of daily, weekly or monthly projects. Depending on the degree of severity of your problem of procrastination, you may only require a "monthly reminder" of your tasks at hand. Here are some helpful tips to perform the task that needs completion:

- *Record Your Goals: Write it Down!* For those who are more chronic in procrastination, perhaps daily (or even hourly) calendar, as shown at the end of the appendix, may be necessary.
- *Realistic Goals: Start Small & Work Up.* Perfection is simply an illusion that we can never attain. Sometimes we build up our expectations of ourselves to the point where we either never begin or we can never complete the project. Start with small tasks and gradually find your pace—what competitive athletes call "finding your zone." Pretend that you are a sculptor and are slowly creating your product—accept the fact that mistakes (and setbacks) are inevitable. Remember the idea of "chipping"—gradual, systematic and progressive behaviors will ultimately result in successful task completion;

- *Relax—Take the Pressure off Yourself! You* set the tone and *you* select the specific environment where you feel that you work best. For example, where do you concentrate and work best? Some people work best while drinking coffee outdoors whereas others work best in a library. Allow a limited amount of time (anywhere from 30 minutes to an hour), relax and begin your work. You will be surprised at how much work can be accomplished in a short and structured period of time.
- *Reward Yourself!* Provide yourself with an incentive or a reason to finish that job or task you have been delaying. Examples may be short-term rewards (i.e., going out to dinner with friends, seeing a movie or just going out) or long-term (planning an exciting vacation later during the year).

Congratulations! You have completed your first step in identifying and resolving the problem of procrastination. You should remember that procrastination never disappears for long—there will always be situations and environments where we may experience "procrastination relapse." Just remember the basic tools that we have described here and you will always have an edge in completing your projects on time.

APPENDIX

WHAT KIND OF PROCRASTINATOR ARE YOU? QUESTIONNAIRE

Answer each of the questions below. Score each answer with either:

1 = Absolutely Not True;

2 = Somewhat Not True;

3 = Not Sure / Don't Know

4 = Somewhat True; and

5 = Absolutely True

1. When I start or begin a project or task, I feel comfortable leaving it unfinished for awhile. _____

2. I usually tend to wait for the "last minute" before I start projects because I need the pressure to do well. _____

3. Sometimes I like to just ignore certain things that I need to do because they tend to go away by themselves. _____

4. I believe that it is much better to wait and give yourself time to do things right rather than to just get started on something. _____

5. I like to do things over and over until they are just perfect—anything less than that to me is unacceptable. _____

6. Sometimes I get so overwhelmed with what needs to be done—I don't know where to start and cannot get started. _____

7. I often tend to underestimate the kinds of things that need to get done as well as how much time it takes to complete a project. _____

8. Usually no one is available (or willing) to help me when I get stuck on a problem and need to finish a project. _____

9. If I don't start or begin a project, I am not that upset because usually someone will volunteer to help besides me. _____

10. I believe that things usually have a way of working themselves out if we just leave things alone. _____

11. I feel that it is better for someone to take their time gradually with a project and delay it rather than running the risk of working too fast and making too many costly errors. _____

12. When I work in group projects, I like to listen to what others have to say and usually wait until someone tells me what to do. _____

13. If I get hungry while right in the middle of an important project, I usually eat first then try to finish whatever it was that I was working on. _____

14. Sometimes when I am working on a project If I cannot make it "just perfect" then I feel like it isn't even worth completing. _____

15. I often feel that people get too "worked up" or anxious over things like due dates and time constraints—I believe that things always tend to work out for the better. _____

16. Sometimes it is better to leave things undone for a while until you know for sure that you are doing something right. _____

17. People who establish goals in their lives are really setting themselves up for failure. _____

18. I tend to avoid making commitments out of fear of breaking them. _____

19. I tend to wait to do the most important things last—I know myself and that I tend to work better under pressure. _____

20. Sometimes I think that it is better not to try something new just to avoid failing at something. _____

21. My supervisor (or teacher at school) at work often tells me to try to get my work in on time. _____

22. Often I am late to many activities and family parties because I can't seem to get started during the day. _____

23. Often I plan many activities to get done on the week-end, but it seems that I never have enough time to get to them. _____

24. I consider myself to be an impulsive person—planning and organization seems to take the fun out of doing things. _____

25. For the most part, I believe we actually can control few things in our lives. If it is "meant to be"—then it will happen to me.

_____

Scoring: Now add up all of your scores and identify what type of procrastinator you are:

125–100: The "Type A"—Chronic Procrastinator. The chronic procrastinator is someone who regularly or consistently delays or avoids meeting deadlines and commitments. The chronic procrastinator is often competitive and tense—often experiencing anxiety over not being able to complete his or her goals. Important projects are seldom completed because the chronic procrastinator has incorporated the maladaptive characteristics of procrastination into a variety of projects in their lives. They engage often in a type of a self-fulfilling prophecy, where they know how important it is to complete a project and at least get started, but they are often preoccupied with minor details that further delay the completion of their project. Often the chronic procrastinator is also a perfectionist—things never get done because things simply are never good enough. The chronic procrastinator finds himself or herself being constantly preoccupied with the smallest details and gradually becoming further and further behind—only to exacerbate the condition. The chronic procrastinator also may engage in perfectionist behavior to avoid his or her fear of failure. The chronic procrastinator may also show a great need for control and becomes so preoccupied with the smallest details that the overall scope and purpose of the project becomes impossible to achieve.

Chronic Procrastinator: 0–25% Completed Project

99–75: The "Type B"–Moderate Procrastinator. In the second category of procrastination, the moderate procrastinator still is unable to achieve his or her goals or meet their deadlines, but they are typically happy and show few signs of stress. Where the type A procrastinator may not achieve goals due to perfectionist ideologies, the type B procrastinator does not achieve his or her goals simply due to a lack of commitment to completing his or her responsibilities. This category of procrastination typically represents an individual who is more focused on having fun and enjoying himself or herself and thus tends to disregard their responsibility. The "Type B" procrastinator typically represents the college student who would rather go out and see a movie than study for an exam the following day. Note that in the relaxed form of procrastination, typically skills and aptitudes exist in order to achieve goals, but a fear of failure exists to even try to achieve goals. It is easier to say you failed at a project or an exam because "you kept putting it off" and therefore didn't really try hard rather than saying you really worked at achieving this goal but still failed;

Moderate Procrastinator: 25–50% Completed Project

74–50: Occasional Procrastinator. The occasional procrastinator shows the most promise in overcoming the problem of procrastination. Occasional procrastinators typically start projects on time and complete the vast majority of what they should be doing. However, often these types of procrastinators leave just a very small amount of work incomplete and thus always have something to do—thereby adding to their list of what needs completion in their lives. With just a small amount of support and structure, occasional procrastinators may easily overcome this habit. The occasional procrastinator can often complete projects but lacks structure and organization in his or her routine. With more structure and the capacity to develop some specific tools to overcome procrastination tendencies they are usually able to set goals and overcome their tendency to put things off.

Occasional Procrastinator:
50–75% Completed Project

49–25: Task Achiever. The task achiever is someone who rarely, if ever, engages in procrastination. The task achiever has excellent time management skills and knows how to organize his or her time effectively. The task achiever also knows how to prioritize—knowing what needs to be done first, second, and so on. The task achiever maximizes most effective use from his or her time and realizes his or her limitations before taking on too many projects. They are usually quite effective in group projects and can help people become motivated as a group in completing projects. Task achievers learn how to maximize their time wisely and complete projects on time. Perhaps most importantly, if the task achiever knows that he or she cannot complete an important task on time, they utilize their support networks and make arrangements to get the task done (note: They do not ask for more time, which is simply an extended form of procrastination).

Task Achiever:
100% Completed Project

Additional Titles in the WESSKA (What Every Student Should Know About . . .) Series:

- What Every Student Should Know About Avoiding Plagiarism   (ISBN 0-321-44689-5)
- What Every Student Should Know About Citing Sources with APA Documentation   (ISBN 0-205-49923-6)
- What Every Student Should Know About Citing Sources with MLA Documentation   (ISBN 0-321-44737-9)
- What Every Student Should Know About Researching Online   (ISBN 0-321-44531-7)
- What Every Student Should Know About Practicing Peer Review   (ISBN 0-321-44848-0)
- What Every Student Should Know About Preparing Effective Oral Presentations   (ISBN 0-205-50545-7)
- What Every Student Should Know About Procrastination (ISBN 0-205-58211-7)
- What Every Student Should Know About Study Skills (ISBN 0-321-44736-0)
- What Every Student Should Know About Reading Maps, Figures, Photographs, and More   (ISBN 0-205-50543-0)

NOTES

NOTES

NOTES

NOTES

NOTES

NOTES

NOTES

NOTES